Boxers

by Grace Hansen

abdopublishing.com

Published by Abdo Kids, a division of ABDO, P.O. Box 398166, Minneapolis, Minnesota 55439.

Copyright © 2017 by Abdo Consulting Group, Inc. International copyrights reserved in all countries.
No part of this book may be reproduced in any form without written permission from the publisher.

Printed in the United States of America, North Mankato, Minnesota.

052016

092016

THIS BOOK CONTAINS
RECYCLED MATERIALS

Photo Credits: iStock, Shutterstock, Thinkstock

Production Contributors: Teddy Borth, Jennie Forsberg, Grace Hansen

Design Contributors: Dorothy Toth, Laura Mitchell

Cataloging-in-Publication Data

Names: Hansen, Grace, author.

Title: Boxers / by Grace Hansen.

Description: Minneapolis, MN : Abdo Kids, [2017] | Series: Dogs. Set 2 | Includes
       bibliographical references and index.

Identifiers: LCCN 2015959085 | ISBN 9781680805154 (lib. bdg.) |
       ISBN 9781680805710 (ebook) | ISBN 9781680806274 (Read-to-me ebook)

Subjects: LCSH: Boxer (Dog breed)--Juvenile literature.

Classification: DDC 636.73--dc23

LC record available at http://lccn.loc.gov/2015959085

Table of Contents

Boxers

Like human boxers, these dogs move **smoothly** and powerfully. They are also fearless!

4

Boxers are medium-sized dogs.

They weigh 60 to 70 pounds

(27 to 32 kg).

Boxers have wrinkled foreheads and **muzzles**. They have dark brown eyes. Their ears naturally lie flat. Some boxers have **cropped** ears.

8

9

Boxers are born with long tails. Some have their tails **docked** after birth.

A boxer's coat is short and shiny. It fits tight on the body.

Boxer coats can be **brindle** or fawn. They can have white markings. All boxers have black masks on their faces.

Grooming

Boxers are clean dogs due to their short coats. They need only an occasional bath. Boxers shed, so brushing them weekly will help. Cleaning their ears is also important.

Exercise & Play

Boxers are very active.

They need lots of exercise.

Boxers love going for long

walks or jogs. They also

enjoy playing fetch.

Personality

Boxers are very smart and easy to train. They are also kind and playful. Boxers are loving members of their families.

21

More Facts

- Boxers are loving and protective, which makes them popular dogs for families.

- The Boxer finds its beginnings in Germany. Its ancestors were made for hunting and holding prey, and later as guard dogs.

- The original reason for Boxers' **docked** tails and **cropped** ears was so the animals they were hunting could not grab onto them. Fewer of today's Boxer owners dock or crop their dogs.

Glossary

brindle – having dark streaks or spots on a gray, tan, or tawny background.

cropped – made to stick straight up.

docked – made to be shorter.

muzzle – part of a dog's face that includes the nose and mouth.

smoothly – even and uninterrupted in flow.

23

Index

abdokids.com

Use this code to log on to abdokids.com and access crafts, games, videos and more!

Abdo Kids Code:
DBK5154